FIRST ON SITE: THE ORIGIN OF A MOBILE DENTAL HYGIENIST

THE BENEFITS OF CONSISTENT DENTAL CARE FOR BABIES AND CHILDREN

1ST EDITION

DEANNA RANDALL ALEXANDER

EDITED BY
PAMELA HILLIARD OWENS

CONTENTS

INTRODUCTION

ABOUT THIS BOOK

I wrote this book to share answers to commonly asked questions or concerns about dental care. It also speaks about my passion for community health, how as a little girl I wanted to become a dental nurse, and how I now share my knowledge of dental care with others. As a 10-year-old, this vision of me in a dream having an ice cream dental truck that would drive around the neighborhood providing dental cleanings and giving away toothbrushes to everyone.

The book begins with questions such as why people don't like the dentist and where that comes from, including the anxiety that causes the resistance that most people share about going to the dentist. When people first see me, the first thing they often say is, "Oh no! I hate the dentist!"

My reply always is, well that good to know because I'm a dental hygienist I'm not the dentist so you're safe with me so far. Then comes the question, what's a real dental emergency? When should I go to the ER for a dental problem? The answer is that severe trauma from a fall or car accident would certainly warrant a dental emergency.

The wisdom teeth section mostly affects teenagers who have a concern about their wisdom teeth and why they hurt so much. I keep biting my cheek or the area becomes abscessed are common complaints.

I recently helped a patient in need of front teeth, the patient would not smile because of the embarrassment of not having front teeth. Once the patient received new teeth replacing the missing teeth, He owned a new attitude about himself and his smile. A person's first impression is when he or she smiles, so when a person can't smile because of dental concerns or missing teeth. It poses a feeling of guilt and shame, my chapter on "Take the Guilt Out of Your Mouth" speaks about dental grills, no front teeth, and or neglect of their teeth and why people don't smile. For the most part, everybody wants a healthy smile and nice teeth. We all can one by "Taking the guilt out of your mouth."

Some people don't want the obligation of maintaining their oral health daily. It may be that they don't have the proper tools for daily maintenance (toothbrush/paste), or they have the "I will do it later" mentality. Because it takes work and daily oral care 2 times daily brushing and dental flossing, and some people don't want to take responsibility. So, they say pull all my teeth and give me a denture then my dental life would be better. Let's talk about that!

Fluoride treatment: the personal choices people make about whether is it necessary or more harm than good.

"Teeth wise Facts about Snacks" talks about making better food choices and how those choices affect our total health both teeth and body.

The story behind access to care is my story about my experiences on the road. Hygiene on Wheels delivers smiles for miles.

ONE

HOW PEOPLE FEEL ABOUT THE DENTIST

Why people don't like the dentist

Many people's fears of the dentist stem from the inherent invasiveness of the process. Whether you're just coming in for a cleaning or a more complex procedure like a root canal, you can't avoid the dentist or hygienist leaning over you and putting their hands right in your mouth.

Nearly half (46%) of all adults aged 30 years or older show signs of gum disease, and severe gum disease affects about 9% of adults. If left untreated, gum disease results in cavities and periodontal disease, which often leads to tooth loss.

Seven out of ten people do not like going to the dentist. More than three out of five (61%) admitted to purposefully putting off an appointment, and it's with good reason. More than half (52%) said they had a bad experience at the dentist.

Anxiety

Many people feel uncomfortable about the physical closeness of the dentist or hygienist to their face. Others may feel self-conscious about the appearance of their teeth or possible mouth odors.

Dental anxiety is most commonly caused by feelings of helplessness, embarrassment, or negative past experiences.

High Cost

Studies show that 75% of people would get the most ideal treatment dentistry has to offer if the cost was not the issue. The most prohibitive thing is the cost of dental treatment. In a capitalist society, healthcare is unfortunately built to be a for-profit venture and people have to choose between their electronic gadgets or healthy teeth.

Sound

The dreaded sound of the drill: 15 % of people avoid the dentist because of this reason. It affects women more than men in general.

The Shots

The actual experience of getting a poke with the needle accounts for 50% of people who hate the dentist. The feeling is something people worry about before the appointment the most. Dreading this part is the most common thing that keeps people away.

Feeling Numb

Studies show that 30% of people hate the feeling of being numb more than the actual injection. The fat lip look or the weird tongue that is half numb...If someone speaks a lot for a living or has a very public job it can be debilitating.

Other Reasons

Oral health professionals and hygienists don't judge because they're happy that you're seeking treatment to improve your oral health. There are many reasons people have the oral health that they have; be it lack of information, no check-ups as a child, socio-economic reasons, or extreme anxiety and shame.

Here are the compiled feelings that dental or hygienist patients might have.

1. "My doctor's hours: M-W 8-5 and Thursday 8-2 with no Fridays, Saturdays, or Sundays! No weeknight or Saturday appointments - he's got it good!"
2. "I seriously dislike getting x-rays and always feeling like I'm gagging."
3. "I don't like questions when I'm being worked on. Only want him to tell stories."

4. "Leaning back in the chair, my stomach gurgles!"
5. "When the tools touch my teeth that are sensitive."
6. "Getting my teeth polished with the gritty polish – it is a texture thing."
7. "Don't like the hygienist whose technique consistently hurts... which is why I request a specific hygienist."
8. "Decor is usually horrible or cutesy tooth-themed."
9. "Getting Novocain shots."
10. "The cost- wish more dentists would barter or trade professional services."
11. "What I hate--EVERYTHING!"
12. "The sounds."
13. "The smells."
14. "Discomfort during cleaning."
15. "Fear of the need for a root canal."
16. "Novocain shots!"
17. "Pricey procedures. Insurance doesn't cover a whole lot of costs."
18. "I get anxious going to the dentist - I think they will find something wrong."
19. "I don't like people in my mouth."
20. "Too personal."
21. "Way too proactive with care (feels like they are looking for things to fix way before they are a problem)."
22. "Scheduling is too far out."
23. "I haven't seen the dentist for very long."
24. "Hate x-rays- always cut my gums on those paper wings."
25. "Getting oversold on things."

Does anyone actually like going to the dentist?
Contrary to the immense fear and dread constantly portrayed in the media about the general public's feelings toward dental visits, many people don't mind going to the dentist, and some even say they genuinely enjoy it!

TWO

DENTAL EMERGENCIES

What's considered a real dental emergency?

Dental emergency classification

Patients who require emergency care are those requiring immediate attention in order to minimize the risk of serious medical complications or prevent long-term dental complications. Their condition means they are most likely to present in Accident & Emergency departments with:

- Uncontrollable dental hemorrhage following extractions
- Rapidly increasing swelling around the throat or eye
- Trauma confined to the dental arches.

Dental unscheduled (or urgent) classification

Patients who require urgent care are those requiring attention for:

- Severe dental and facial pain not controlled by over-the-counter preparations
- Dental and soft tissue acute infection

Non-urgent dental conditions

A number of individuals currently access care out-of-office (OOS) services who are not in pain and present for treatment regarding non-urgent problems.

These may include:

- Patients not in pain
- Aesthetic problems (dislodged crowns and bridges)
- Patients with broken dentures
- Patients with hospital referral letters
- Patients requiring permanent restorations
- Non-traumatic problems with orthodontic appliances
- Patients who have no significant pathology
- Patients requiring a second opinion
- Patients using EDS as their regular dentist
- Requiring surgical extractions (wisdom teeth) and are not in pain

THREE

WHAT TO KNOW ABOUT WISDOM TEETH

Facts About Wisdom Teeth

- **How to know if you have wisdom teeth.**

In many people, wisdom teeth don't break through the gum and grow out, or only part of them do. Most young adults have at least one wisdom tooth that hasn't broken through. This is more common in the lower jaw than it is in the upper jaw. The reason is usually that there isn't enough room in the jaw. Other teeth may then get in the way of the wisdom tooth, or the wisdom tooth might come in crooked.

- **Everyone has wisdom teeth.**

Wisdom teeth that don't break through (sometimes also called "impacted" wisdom teeth) often don't cause any problems. But they sometimes lead to pain, swelling, tooth decay, or inflamed gums. Impacted wisdom teeth may also push other teeth out of the way. Wisdom teeth that break through the gums may or may not cause problems too.

Because early humans needed to chew coarse, hearty foods, they required a broader jaw, and wisdom teeth grew in to give them more chewing power. Because the jaw was wider, the wisdom teeth were able to grow in with no difficulties.

- **Wisdom teeth have no purpose.**

These days, most of the food we eat is cut up and cooked, making it easy to chew. These new eating habits caused our jaws to narrow, leaving no room for wisdom teeth. Over time, our jawbones have evolved to be much smaller, meaning that all 32 teeth can no longer fit in our mouths. For this reason, wisdom teeth now need to be extracted when they erupt, usually between ages 17 and 21. These teeth can become impacted and cause many issues, especially because they are so far back in the mouth that adequately cleaning them can be a problem, even if they grow in with no issues.

- **Why wisdom teeth may need to be removed.**

The problems associated with wisdom teeth are pain, trapping food, and debris behind the wisdom tooth causing infection or gum disease (periodontal disease). Tooth decay in a partially erupted wisdom tooth can cause damage to a nearby tooth or surrounding bone. The development of a fluid-filled sac (cyst) around the wisdom tooth is also of concern. Along with complications with orthodontic treatments to straighten other teeth.

An impacted wisdom tooth may grow at an angle toward the next tooth (second molar) or grow at an angle toward the back of the mouth. It can also grow in at a right angle to the other teeth as if the wisdom tooth is "lying down" within the jawbone. Wisdom teeth can grow straight up or down like other teeth but stay trapped within the jawbone.

FOUR

INFORMATION ABOUT DENTAL TOOLS

Dental Floss

Dental floss is a cord of thin filaments used to clean in between your teeth and remove food and dental plaque in places a toothbrush has difficulty reaching. Floss should be regularly used as part of a daily oral cleaning regime and assists in maintaining good oral health.

Flossing helps lift and release food and plaque stuck in between your teeth. While brushing removes these particles from your mouth, if you brush first and floss afterward, food and plaque remain in your mouth until the next time you brush.

If you can use string floss, you should always choose it over floss picks. String floss cleans more effectively than picks because you can move it to make that all-important "C" shape that gets up close to the gum line. String floss also allows you to use a fresh section for each tooth.

Benefits of flossing:

- Removal of plaque from below the gum line, which can erode tooth enamel and develop into tartar and cause tooth discoloration.
- Reduce the risk of cavities.

There are plenty of safe dental floss options to choose from. Instead of nylon floss, look for floss made of natural silk which is biodegradable. If you prefer nylon floss, look for one that is coated in something other than petroleum. Beeswax is a popular alternative.

According to the American Dental Association (ADA), interdental cleaners such as floss are an essential part of taking care of your teeth and gums.

Cleaning between teeth removes plaque that can lead to cavities or gum disease in the areas where a toothbrush can't reach.

When floss was invented:

Floss as we know it today was developed around 200 years ago. In 1815, an American dentist named Levi Spear Parmly introduced the idea of using waxen silk thread as floss.

However, it wasn't until the mid-20th century that flossing became more widespread. During World War II, Dr. Charles C. Bass, known as "The Father of Preventive Dentistry," developed nylon floss, noting that it was more elastic and durable than silk. After the war, flossing became much more mainstream.

Why dental floss may smell bad:

A regular bad smell or taste after flossing could indicate that there is a dental problem, especially if breath smells less than pleasant at other times.

Does floss remove tartar?

Unfortunately, tartar can only be removed by your dental hygienist and/or dentist with dental instruments or an ultrasonic scaling device, however, using dental floss once a day is a great step toward preventing plaque buildup.

Does floss have an expiration date?

Dental floss does not expire; only the flavor can start lessening after a long period. The exception is if the dental floss has other materials with a designated shelf life. In that case, it's advised to monitor the expiration date and take a closer look at the materials that make up the floss.

Flossing Aids and Tools: Flossing with braces and under bridgework

Water flossing offers a simple way to floss without thin floss thread. This type of handheld device removes plaque by spraying streams of water between the teeth. The steady pressure of water directed to the space between each tooth effectively targets food debris, sugar, bacteria, and other substances.

Interdental Brushes: Like tiny toothbrushes, specially designed to clean between your teeth, these brushes are a great alternative to flossing. Interdental brushes are usually easier to use than a thread of floss, are just as effective as floss, and are probably your best option if you have braces.

Floss threaders are rigid, yet flexible pieces of plastic that assist in passing dental floss around fixed bridgework, behind orthodontic wires, and under denture retainer bars. Floss threaders resemble large 'needles,' and are incredibly effective in passing dental floss between teeth that are connected. Many threaders are reusable, but others are disposable.

You should use a floss threader if:

- You wear braces.
- You have a permanent retainer.
- You are in the process of having bridgework done.
- You need to reach spaces under the dental retainer bars.
- You have dental appliances that prevent your ability to floss into the gum line of each tooth. Floss threaders offer the next best solution for receiving the best possible dental health. Because flossing is such an important part of your dental routine, be sure to floss at least once a day, regardless of which dental appliance you use to prevent plaque build-up and tooth decay.

FIVE

TAKE THE GUILT OUT OF YOUR MOUTH

When You're Afraid

This is called dental anxiety, which is characterized by uneasiness or exaggerated fears about going to the dentist. It also includes being embarrassed to go to the dentist because of the state of your mouth, how your teeth look, and more.

Gap Teeth, No Teeth, Missing Teeth

Your bite exerts tremendous pressure, as much as 168 pounds at your second molar, and the total bite pressure is about 5600 pounds per square inch. Your teeth are well-equipped to deal with the bite pressure itself. Actually, teeth are able to resist a compressive force of about 30,000 pounds.

Your tooth enamel isn't made up of a single piece of enamel, but numerous tiny rods of enamel that are stacked up beside one another. At the outside of the tooth, these rods are parallel, but down deep in the tooth, these rods are wound together. So, although your teeth are designed to withstand some serious forces, they shouldn't be put under the extra stress of using them in ways that can increase the existence of micro cracks.

This means you should avoid using your teeth to chew on hard things like ice, pens, or other non-foods, and wear a mouthguard whenever you're at risk of a blow from contact sports. If you experience bruxism, you should get it treated to reduce the stress it puts on your teeth.

False Teeth Dentures and Partial Dentures (with the metal clasp)

Should you save your teeth or extract them for dentures?

It is usually best to save healthy natural teeth. When your natural teeth are healthy, it won't compromise your oral health. Replacing teeth with a removable appliance- a partial denture or full denture has its disadvantages. The denture can move or slide if not anchored, and won't be comfortable.

Some factors to consider the factors to help you decide if you want to keep your teeth or get a full denture set:

- When there are a few teeth remaining, they are under a lot of stress from chewing and eating. If you only have upper teeth that are healthy, the force from your lower teeth when you bite and chew puts stress on the upper teeth. Pressure on the teeth can weaken them internally, even if they appear fine on the outside.
- Full upper dentures offer increased comfort, the suction keeps a full upper denture in place, and it moves less than a lower denture. It's easier to eat and chew with it. A well-made upper denture is healthy for other teeth, and it's more gentle on lower teeth.
- When all your teeth are missing, your jawbone is affected. Teeth stimulate the jawbone so when all teeth are missing, the stimulation stops, and your body resorbs the bone. After 10 to 20 years, you'll lack enough jawbone to support your facial muscles, and your face will sag and make you look older. The missing bone will make it difficult,- if not impossible, to keep a lower denture in place.

Cosmetic Grills, Gold Front Teeth, and Dental Crowns

Grills are not recommended because they could pose a problem to your oral health and hygiene. By wearing grills, you might increase your risk of tooth decay and gum disease. This is because bacterial plaque can get trapped between them and the tooth's surface.

Acids can cause tooth decay and harm gum tissue. Bacteria may also contribute to bad breath. There also is the potential for grills to irritate surrounding oral tissues and to wear the enamel away on the opposing teeth. To prevent problems, limit the amount of time spent wearing removable grills.

Whether you want to enhance your appearance or restore a smile that has been damaged by severe staining, decay, or an injury, crowns are excellent options. They are available in a variety of materials and styles, and when crowns are placed on the teeth, they restore and protect your smile in a truly effective manner.

Bonding a gold material directly to your teeth may seem like a dangerous idea. In some instances, this bonding can harm the teeth. However, the bonding process is conducted in the safest, most effective manner possible, so there is no risk of tooth damage.

After a full exam and consultation, the 22-karat gold crowns are placed onto the teeth. This process uses a permanent cement to affix the gold crowns to the tooth, which protects the teeth from any damage.

Most people are surprised to learn that the use of gold in dentistry dates back 4,000 years. Gold was used to fill in blackened, decayed, or discolored teeth. Of course, only the wealthy and most important individuals were able to use gold, so gold teeth became known as symbols of wealth, power, and status.

If you are experiencing the following, you are most likely a great candidate for gold crowns:

- Discolored or severely stained teeth
- Damaged or decayed tooth
- Misshapen teeth

In addition, gold crowns can be used to protect an unhealthy tooth that is at risk of fracturing.

Lastly, gold crowns are ideal for anyone who wants to restore their smile in a custom and stylish manner that will stand the test of time.

Maintenance of Gold Crowns

Many people believe gold is too difficult to maintain. While it is a precious metal, gold is incredibly durable, so maintaining the crowns while maintaining your oral health will not be as overwhelming as people think.

Brushing and flossing as normal is recommended. Make sure you brush your teeth and gold crowns twice a day. Use a soft-bristled brush to protect your tooth enamel, gum tissue, and the gold used in your crowns.

Schedule routine checkups with your dentist/hygienist-even after you have your gold crowns. Again, gold is a durable material, but the crowns are not meant to last a lifetime. With proper care, you can expect your gold crowns to last at least 10 years.

Bucked teeth, Crooked teeth, Discolored teeth, Big Teeth

There are several causes of buck teeth including genetics, missing teeth, impacted teeth, extra teeth, thumb sucking, or even using a pacifier too long. Tongue thrusting is also another common cause. Our smile is a significant part of our personality, and having twisted, overlapping, or crooked teeth can immensely affect our confidence.

Common Causes of Bucked Teeth

Thumb Sucking: the pressure from the thumb consistently applied to the still-growing gums causes the teeth to grow in crooked, especially outwards.

Tongue Thrusting: causes misaligned teeth, especially an overbite, i.e., protruding upper teeth. Misaligned teeth or malocclusion is caused when the size of the upper or lower jaw is smaller than usual.

Genetics: Children often get crooked teeth from their parents. Facial trauma, such as a jaw injury in childhood, can also result in displaced teeth or misaligned bites.

Problems Associated with Bucked or Crooked Teeth

Gum Disease Wear and Tear: excessive wear and tear leads to TMJ disorder or Temporomandibular Jaw disorder where the patients experience extreme pain or even locking of the jaw bone on movement.

Difficulty Chewing: which can lead to digestion problems.

Speech Difficulty: problems pronouncing a few words, which is a common result of crooked teeth.

Low Self-Esteem: this also results in poor dental health, which can result in stained teeth that look unappealing and make people feel embarrassed.

What to look for when trying to find a dentist or dental hygiene services--positive and negative signs:

If the practice is being run by a business person, not a medical or dental professional, this is normally a sign of millwork dentistry.

If the clinic maximizes the billing of insurance companies over helping people.

If patients are being taught how to reverse their gum disease (an essential first step before ANY work is done).

Skipping past the gum disease and cavities straight to the big-ticket items such as veneers, whitening, and so on, is not a sign of care for the patient.

SIX

FLUORIDE AND DENTAL CLEANINGS

How fluoride works

- Fluoride reduces the solubility of enamel in acid by converting hydroxyapatite into less soluble fluorapatite; it may also exert an influence directly on dental plaque, reducing the ability of plaque organisms to produce acid, and it promotes the remineralization of tooth enamel in areas that have been decalcified by acids.
- Fluoride joins the tooth structure when teeth develop, thus strengthening the teeth' enamel, making them less susceptible to bacteria and cavities. Fluoride slows and may even reverse the development of decay and cavities by harming the bacteria that cause cavities.
- Fluoride treatments at the dentist is very important, and people should get one at least every year. Typically, tap water in the US contains fluoride, and most toothpaste manufacturers also add fluoride as an ingredient in their toothpaste.
- For all-around protection (and not just cavity prevention), stannous fluoride is the preferred fluoride of choice. Sodium

fluoride alone isn't enough for optimum tooth decay prevention.

More Facts About Fluoride

- Fluoride is a mineral that occurs naturally and is released from rocks into the soil, water, and air. Almost all water contains some fluoride, but usually not enough to prevent tooth decay. Fluoride can also be added to drinking water supplies as a public health measure for reducing cavities.
- The most common fluoride compound used in mouth rinses is sodium fluoride. The fluoride from mouth rinse is retained in dental plaque and saliva and helps prevent tooth decay.
- Fluoride helps prevent tooth decay by making the tooth more resistant to acid attacks from plaque bacteria and sugars in the mouth. It also reverses early decay.
- Fluorosis stains won't go away with brushing and flossing. The only way to get rid of fluorosis is with cosmetic dental treatments like dental bonding, veneers, or crowns.
- Fluoride varnish is a dental treatment that can help prevent tooth decay, slow it down, or stop it from getting worse.
- Fluoride varnish is made with fluoride, a mineral that can strengthen tooth enamel (outer coating on teeth). Fluoride varnish treatments cannot completely prevent cavities.
- Fluoride varnish protects teeth for several months. It works best if it is reapplied every three to six months.

The Benefits of Fluoride for Oral Health

- Fluoride kills bacteria that cause cavities & gum disease. It's also antimicrobial, which means it can kill the bacteria that contribute to cavities and gum disease.
- According to the World Health Organization (WHO), fluoride is one of the very few chemicals that has been shown to result in significant positive results for people who drink fluoridated water.

- Drinking fluoridated water also keeps teeth strong and reduces cavities and tooth decay by about 25% in children and adults.
- Fluoride treatment regimens have been developed to prevent dental caries. Systemic fluoride is easily absorbed and is taken into the enamel during the period of pre-eruptive tooth formation. The primary beneficial cariostatic effects of fluoride in erupted teeth occur locally at the tooth surface.
- Since 1950, the American Dental Association (ADA) has stated that fluoride is safe, effective, and necessary in preventing tooth decay. By strengthening enamel and slowing its breakdown, fluoride limits the ability of plaque and bacteria to damage your teeth.
- Fluoride treatments are typically professional treatments containing a high concentration of fluoride that a dentist or hygienist will apply to a person's teeth to improve dental health and reduce the risk of cavities. These in-office treatments may take the form of a solution, gel, foam, or varnish.
- In medically recommended doses, receiving fluoride treatments during pregnancy is a safe and effective preventive measure for your oral health.

Fluoride Applications in Dentistry

- **Silver Diamine Fluoride:** Of all the options for treating cavities and tooth decay in toddlers and children, silver diamine fluoride (SDF) is the least invasive and an alternative to classic fillings.

The disadvantages of SDF include potential pupal and oral soft tissue irritation and dental staining. Attention is needed during the application to avoid contact of the solution with the gingiva, since it may cause irritation.

- **Silver Nitrate:** Silver nitrate (SN) is most commonly used as a non-invasive treatment option, especially in children or the elderly.

SN has been used for several years in dentistry.

- The earliest known use of silver nitrate in a dental setting was in the year 1000 AD, in feudal Japan. Silver nitrate and silver diamine fluoride are commonly used to halt decay and the growth of cavities.

SEVEN

EDUCATING ABOUT DENTAL CARE IN CHILDREN

Several studies have been completed about the importance of dental health care education. More information about the studies is available in the References chapter.

Dental caries is the most common chronic disease of children in the United States, with a prevalence of 41% among children ages 2 through 11 [1].

Oral health and dental care are important for young children because sound oral function is required for eating, speech development, and the emergence of a positive self-image. Negative oral and dental conditions can predispose children to significant oral problems.

Dietary advice given for general development and well-being needs to be integrated into oral health counseling.

Oral hygiene contributes to caries prevention in young children. The U.S. Surgeon General's conference highlighted the access to dental care problems for children. An estimated 52 million school hours a year are lost by children due to dental oral concerns [4].

Proper education on what to eat in combination with oral examinations and radiographs helps determine any contributing diet/nutritional factors to oral manifestations or disease, as well as the impact of the sensory and functional status of the oral cavity [5].

The objective of one study was to determine parent's knowledge and attitudes about the importance of early dental intervention and nutrition in young children.

The majority of those surveyed agreed that children should have their first dental check-up at 1 year of age and that children should visit the dentist by 2 years of age.

Our intentions were to raise awareness of early dental prevention and care for young children. There is a growing awareness of early dental care and proper nutritional education for young children. Parents and dental professionals should be actively involved in the health care and maintenance of young children.

We assessed, using a survey, the parents' knowledge and attitudes regarding early dental care in the first and second years of life. My results on early intervention are similar to other studies. The American Academy of Pediatric Dentistry Association, American Public Health Association, Association of State of and Territorial Dental Directors, California Dental Association, and California Society of Pediatric Dentists currently recommend that children receive their first dental evaluation within the first year of life (6).

Getting children the dental care they need is often a problem due to barriers associated with public and private dental delivery systems. However, the barriers to care may also be due to parents' skills and social support, which is an important part of positive oral health behavior. Trends in early intervention for preschool children are the result of low early childhood caries prevalence with early intervention, which reduces early childhood disease (8).

The early start of oral health programs will have significant benefits on the effects of caries prevention. Emphasis on the importance of good nutritional habits, along with regular dental visits.

It appears that diet remains the key factor in the caries process. Certain feeding practices, such as bedtime bottle feeding, "at will" breastfeeding, and frequent intake of sugary snacks and drinks contribute to the development of early childhood cavities.

Early intervention is a fast-growing awareness for early dental care and proper nutrition awareness for young children. This information is valuable to dental professionals and caregivers. Its emphasis is on the prevention of dental problems rather than the restorative care (6).

Parents and dental professionals should be actively involved in the dental health care of preschool children.

EIGHT

THE STORY BEHIND ACCESS TO DENTAL CARE AND PREVENTION OF DECAY AND CAVITIES WITH A MOBILE DENTIST HYGIENIST PRACTICE

The American Academy of Pediatric Dentistry (AAPD) recognizes that infant oral health is one of the foundations upon which preventive education and dental care must be built to enhance the opportunity for a lifetime free from preventable oral disease.

Good oral hygiene habits early in life can lead to lifelong good oral health. There are new state regulations allowing the practice of non-traditional dental clinics to bring much-needed assistance in providing access to care starting with the infant population.

Providing early assessment for our young children, prior to the start of school, can close the gap in the fight against early childhood tooth decay. Caring for these little teeth is an essential foundation for good oral health for when the permanent teeth start emerging.

The barriers to receiving care are often magnified by no insurance or qualified knowledge of the importance of early risk assessment before the age of 3.

If this problem continues to go unaddressed it will lead to rampant decay, premature missing teeth, or other medical-related illnesses.

Access to dental care plays a vital role in determining whether a child experiences oral pain. In addition to the relationship between toothaches, dental insurance, and socioeconomic status, strong links existed between toothaches, annual dental visits, and difficulty obtaining dental care.

The goal is to ensure that uninsured and underserved children have access to oral healthcare services and to prevention awareness by providing early assessments, coronal polishing, toothbrushes, flossing instructions, and dental referral services when needed to the parents.

Early assessment is an important issue surrounding early prevention and oral hygiene education.

With the inception of mobile dental hygiene services, the benefits have included increased visibility in reaching more of the underserved population that is in desperate need of assistance and access to dental care.

Hygiene on Wheels (H.O.W) is operated by a licensed Dental Hygienist who is looking to close the gap in dental assessments for children 0-36 months before the eruption of their primary teeth. H.O.W is a non-profit organization formed in 2008 using a state-of-the-art mobile dental unit.

It is presently offering free prevention awareness workshops for the citizens of Detroit who are homebound and require services in their homes or facilities. The mission is to ensure that the community is aware of the importance of early dental assessment for children prior to school age.

Outreach learning programs, together with activities in the community provide workshops on dental awareness and supply product samples to spread the word about early caries detection. Community service means providing a service to a group within a community, this service may include clinical dental hygiene, education, or projects that promote healthy behavior.

Being involved in community service is a tremendous opportunity for dental hygienists to promote healthy behavior and prevention to provide care to the entire community and to allow dental hygienists to use their abilities and skills to help others. Dental health educational programs strive to provide preventive dental health tools to large populations.

By providing the care needed to keep a smile healthy and give the best possible service and results, dental hygienists are committed to continual education and learning. They attend dental lectures, meetings, and dental conventions to stay informed of new techniques, the latest products, and the newest equipment that a modern dental office can utilize to provide state-of-the-art dental care.

H.O.W is a mobile dental operation providing "Into the mouths of

Babes, Oral care protocol for babies and expecting mothers." An oral care education and awareness program is offered to the Metro-Detroit communities, focusing on expecting mothers and infants 0-36 months and introducing oral hygiene regimes, dental assessments, and dental cleanings through prevention awareness plans that establish measures to help prevent early childhood decay.

H.O.W. aims to improve the oral health of children by starting with babies and their parents or caregivers. There is a sense of urgency to provide early assessments to infants along with raising dental education awareness to the expecting mothers to combat early disease detection before decay starts.

Dental disease can be inherited from the mother and passed to the child. Education is a vital step in the promotion and detection of early oral disease detection and prevention for the expecting mother and their baby.

Into the Mouths of Babes is one of the many programs offered by Hygiene on Wheels, which aims to deliver preventive oral care health awareness. Educating expecting mothers on the necessity of early oral evaluations, oral risk assessments, and proper oral care for infants prior to the eruption of teeth is important.

The goal is to make major impacts in the prevention and reduction of early childhood decay. It is very important to have proper oral hygiene and good dietary habits, for caries prevention which proves to be the most important strategy for the prevention of early childhood decay.

Providing children the dental care they need is often a problem due to a few barriers associated with public and private dental delivery systems. The parents don't always have adequate knowledge of how to prevent oral disease. However, the barriers to care are also often due to parents' skills and social support, which is an important part of positive oral health behavior.

Trends in early intervention for preschool children are the result of low early childhood caries prevalence with early intervention, which reduces early childhood disease (Decker 2004) and improves oral health in infants and toddlers, by educating parents and caregivers through workshops and understanding the disease processes that can affect infants.

Merging Medical and Dental Programs

The importance of collaboration of the medical and dental industry on a crusade to service the underserved or uninsured begins with the children. We must deliver preventive oral health services to high-risk children insured by Medicaid.

Education and awareness services should be provided from the time of the first tooth eruption until age 3½ (42 months), including regular oral evaluations and risk assessment, fluoride varnish applications, and referral to a dental home as needed.

The relationship between nutrition and oral health is addressed in the United States Public Health Services Healthy People 2010 objectives for the nation, which address the prevention and management of oral and craniofacial conditions (Decker 2004).

Dental practitioners, like other health care providers, can provide nutrition education as a component of comprehensive care. This is important information at the forefront of early intervention for both the parent and the child regarding the need for early oral care assessments before the disease starts.

Oral hygiene is a major factor when it comes to caries prevention in young children. One of the strengths of the Hygiene on Wheels "Into the Mouth of Babes" programs is that we are joining a fast-growing awareness for early dental care and proper nutrition awareness for young children, especially when coupled with emerging research demonstrating a stronger association between oral health and overall systemic health. This information is valuable, and its emphasis is on the prevention of dental problems rather than restorative care.

ABOUT THE AUTHOR

ABOUT THE AUTHOR

De'Anna Randall-Alexander R.D.H. M.A, B.S., A.S

DeAnna Alexander holds a Bachelor of Science Degree in Dental Hygiene, and a master's Degree in Liberal Studies from the University of Detroit Mercy School Liberal Studies. She has over 30+ years of clinical experience, a friendly demeanor, and a gentle touch. She has earned consistent praise from patients and employers.

She is a Healthcare provider for Hygiene on Wheels, a community outreach program, which she began in 2008. The program provides oral hygiene education and dental care to underserved populations. The mission of Hygiene on Wheels focuses on being viable in the community to educate the public about preventive dental health care and offer resources for additional care.

In addition, DeAnna puts together activities with other organizations to assist in providing care to kids in need of dental healthcare services. She is presently formulating a program designed to provide oral health advocacy in the classroom, which will be directed to schools and after-school programs. She understands the difficulties associated with access to care for the underserved. With excitement and enthusiasm, she looks forward to working with the elderly to provide much-needed services and care to the senior population.

In her spare time, she enjoys music, cooking, and spending time with her 14-year-old son.

Deanna Alexander is one of the Michigan dental health providers selected to receive a custom mobile dental clinic through the Motor City Kares initiative – a $500,000 initiative aimed at uplifting minority businesses and bringing high-quality, mobile oral health care services to communities and residents in Southwest Detroit.

Hygiene on Wheels, Inc. received a custom Ford Transit van converted into a mobile dental office later this year. The mobile units will be equipped with technology – including digital x-rays, intraoral cameras, tele-dentistry capabilities, and more – that allow the businesses to provide preventative dental care and dental hygiene education to insured, uninsured, and under-insured patients alike.

Mobile Dentistry is an innovative way of delivering dental hygiene care to the community. The busy lifestyle of millennials is a reason for them to ignore their oral hygiene. Seniors with mobility issues also find it hard to get their regular dental hygiene care needs met. Visiting their home or business helps them overcome this excuse. Mobile healthcare service delivery is the future as lifestyles are getting busier.

Deanna has spent her career in private practice and dental education at both the university and community college levels. Deanna has served as Adjunct Dental Assistant Instructor for Dorsey Career School. Deanna earned her education specialist in Dental Hygiene from Wayne County Community College and her Bachelor's in Dental Hygiene and Master's degree in Liberal Studies and Education from the University of Detroit Mercy. She has a broad background in education; a strong history of success in strategic planning and making contributions to the establishment of collaborative healthcare programs; and extensive experience with program outcomes assessment and use of data for improvement and the implementation of service-learning programs and community outreach.

BIBLIOGRAPHY

REFERENCES

1. Berkowitz RJ. Causes, treatment, and prevention of early childhood caries: A microbiologic perspective. *J Can Dent Assoc.* (2003); 69:304-7.
2. Dye BA, Tan S, Smith V, et al. Trends in oral health status: United States, 1988-1994 and 1999-2004. National Center for Health Statistics Vital Health Stat (2007); 11(248).
3. Edelstein BL. J Public Health Dent Access to Dental Care for Head Start enrollees.
4. (2000)(3):22- 9.
5. Henry J. Kaiser Foundation, Oral Health in the U.S.: Key Facts (June 2012).
6. Michigan Department of Education, Head Start Program website (2015) State of Michigan.
7. Pierce KM, Rozier RG, Vann WF Jr. Accuracy of pediatric primary care providers' screening and referral for early childhood caries. *Pediatrics* (2002); 109(5): E82-2.
8. Ramos-Gomez f, Jue B, Bonta Cy. J California Dental Association Implementing an infant care program. (2002) (10):752-61.
9. Riva Touger-Decker. Quintessence International Role of Nutrition in the Dental Practice (2004).
10. U.S. Dept. of Health and Human Services. Oral health in America: A report of the Surgeon General. Rockville, Maryland: US Dept. of Health and Human Services, National Institute of Dental and Craniofacial Research, National Institutes of Health; (2000).
11. David T. Ozar, Ph.D., FACD David J. Sokol, DDS, JD, FACD Dental Ethics at Chairside, Social Justice and Access to Dental care, 219-231.
12. Wendy E. Mouradian "Ethical principle and the delivery of children's oral health care" MDM.
13. Dela Cruz Rozier RG Slade G Pediatric 2004 Nov; 114 (5):e642-52; Dental screening and referral of young children by pediatric primary care providers.
14. Edelstein BL Spec-Care Dentist 2002:223 (Supp;) : 11S-25S Dental care considerations for young children.
15. Edelstein BL Ambul Pediatric., 2002 Mar-Apr (Suppl) 141-7 Dental care considerations for young children.
16. www.slate.com/articles Health September 5, 2013, 2013 Why are not dead yet.